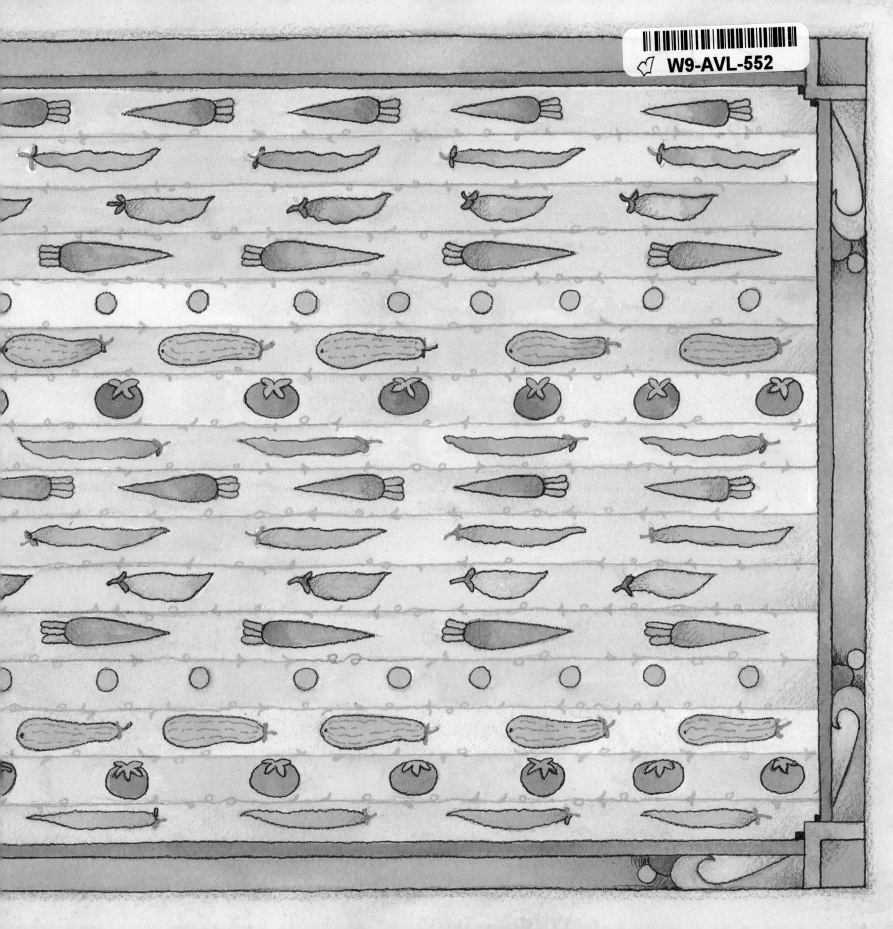

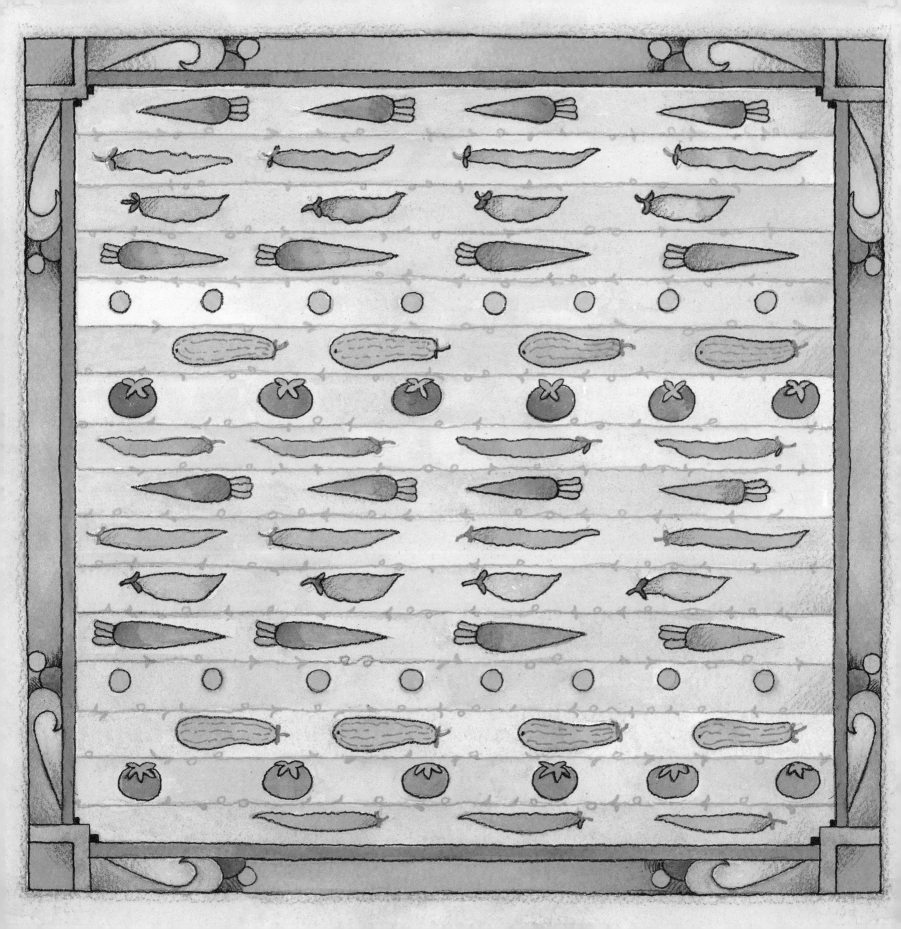

Making Minestrone

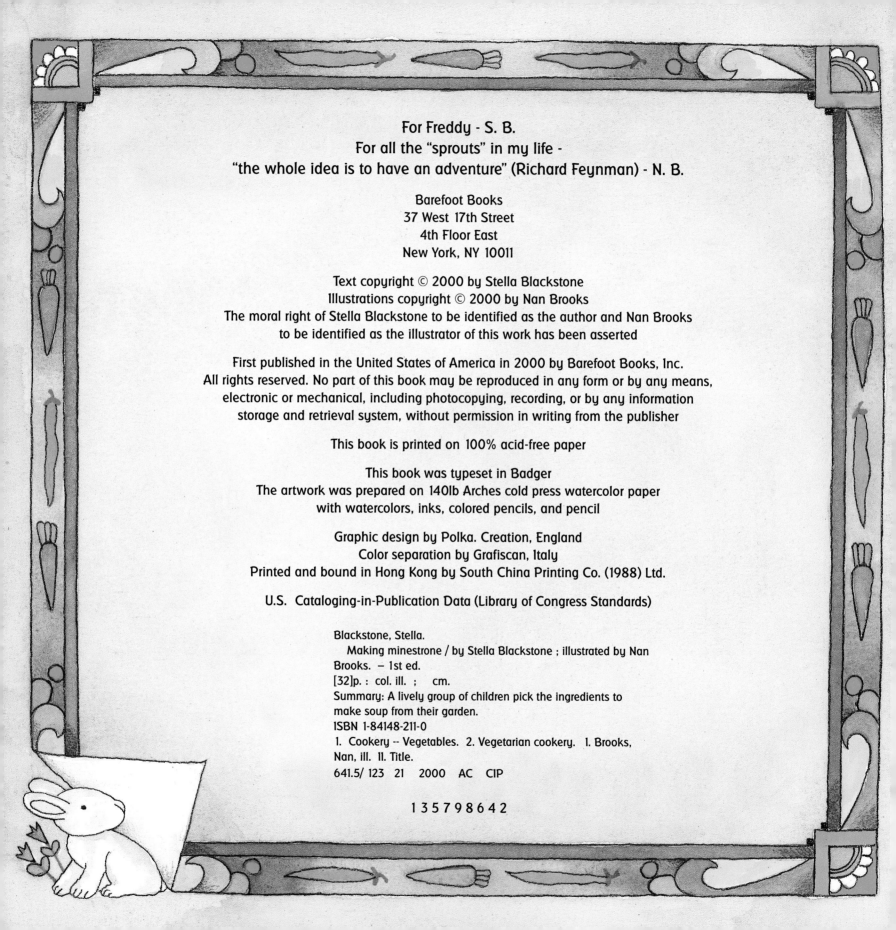

For Freddy - S. B.
For all the "sprouts" in my life -
"the whole idea is to have an adventure" (Richard Feynman) - N. B.

Barefoot Books
37 West 17th Street
4th Floor East
New York, NY 10011

This book is printed on 100% acid-free paper

This book was typeset in Badger
The artwork was prepared on 140lb Arches cold press watercolor paper
with watercolors, inks, colored pencils, and pencil

Graphic design by Polka. Creation, England
Color separation by Grafiscan, Italy
Printed and bound in Hong Kong by South China Printing Co. (1988) Ltd.

U.S. Cataloging-in-Publication Data (Library of Congress Standards)

Blackstone, Stella.
    Making minestrone / by Stella Blackstone ; illustrated by Nan
Brooks. – 1st ed.
[32]p. : col. ill. ;   cm.
Summary: A lively group of children pick the ingredients to
make soup from their garden.
ISBN 1-84148-211-0
1. Cookery -- Vegetables. 2. Vegetarian cookery. 1. Brooks,
Nan, ill. II. Title.
641.5/ 123 21   2000 AC CIP

1 3 5 7 9 8 6 4 2

Making Minestrone

written by **Stella Blackstone**

illustrated by **Nan Brooks**

walk
the way of wonder...
Barefoot Books

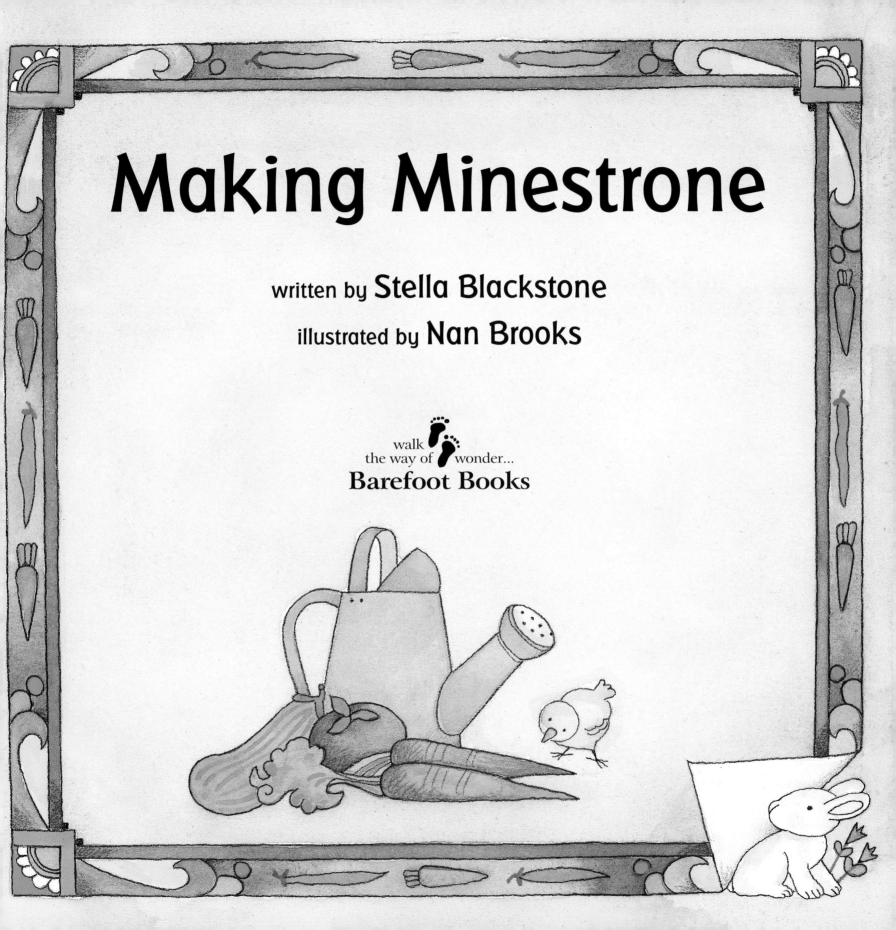

What do you do when you're feeling lonely?
You ask all your friends around to make a minestrone!

You need:

Green Beans   *Zucchini*

Carrots   *Pasta*

Onions   *Cooking oil*

Peas   *Salt & pepper*

Potatoes   *Water*

7

Each take a basket to carry what you pick,
And hurry to the garden — quick, quick, quick!

9

Here are the tomatoes, juicy, round, and red.

And here are the potatoes, deep inside their bed.

Over there are onions – they will make you cry!

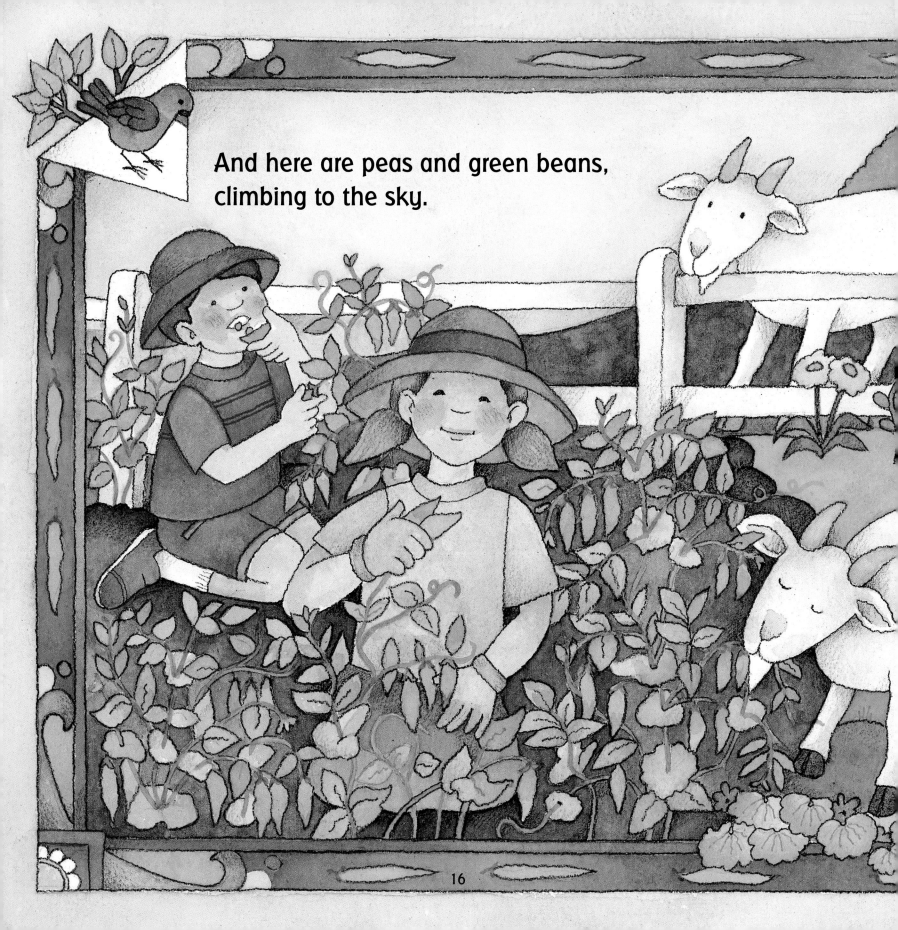

And here are peas and green beans,
climbing to the sky.

Zucchini have enormous leaves, furry, wide, and flat,

Carrot leaves are feathery – rabbits all know that!

20

Is everybody ready? Let's start to cook!

23

Wash, peel, slice, chop!
Then fry up the onions in a great big pot.

25

Stir in all the vegetables,
Lots of water too,
Salt and pepper, pasta shells,
A wish for me and you.

Bubble, bubble, bubble!
Quickly lay the table!

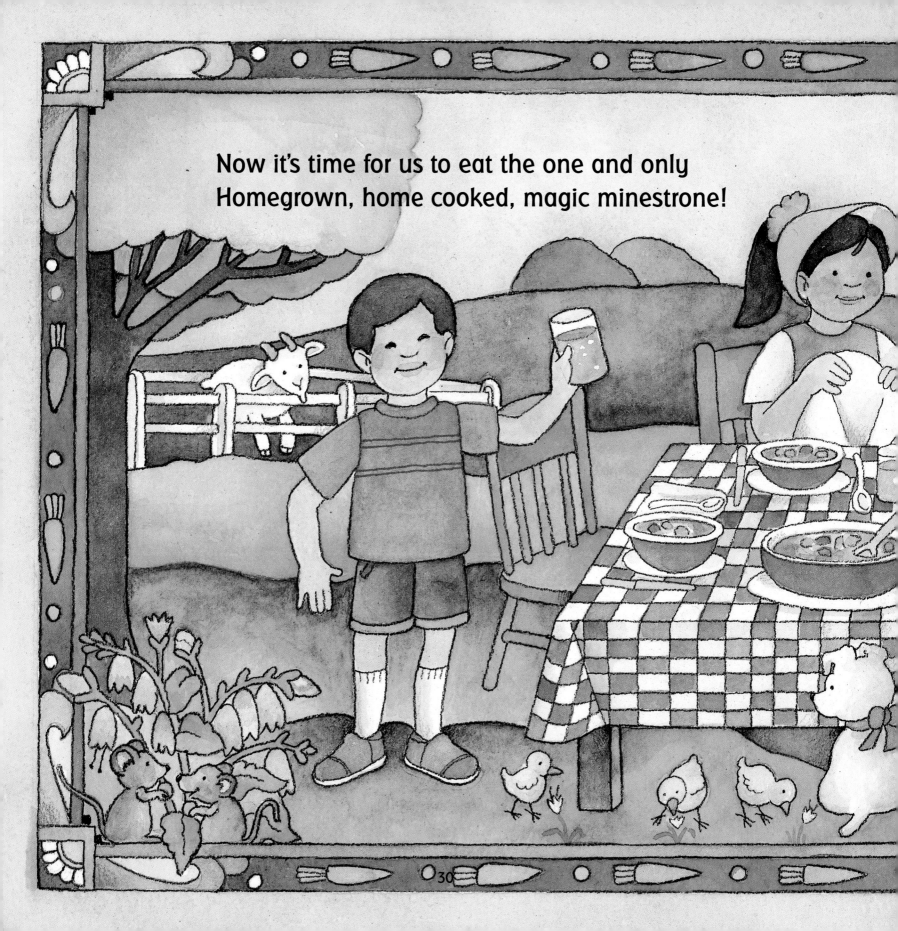

Now it's time for us to eat the one and only
Homegrown, home cooked, magic minestrone!

How to Make a Minestrone

(Serves 4)

1 tablespoon olive oil
1 onion, peeled and chopped
1-2 cloves garlic, crushed
1 large carrot, peeled and diced
5 cups vegetable stock
6 tomatoes, chopped (or half a can)
1 large potato, peeled and diced
$\frac{1}{2}$ can cannellini beans
$\frac{1}{2}$ cup small pasta shapes
$\frac{1}{2}$ cup fresh or frozen peas (or half a can)
$1\frac{1}{2}$ cups cabbage, chopped
1 cup green beans, chopped
1 medium zucchini, chopped
2 tablespoons chopped parsley
2 tablespoons pesto
salt and pepper

Sauté the onion and garlic in the oil for about 10 minutes until golden brown.
Add the carrot and fry for 2 minutes. Add the stock, tomatoes, potato, cannellini beans,
pasta, and fresh peas (if using). Bring to boil, reduce the heat, half cover the pan with the
lid and simmer for 40 minutes. Add the canned or frozen peas (if using), cabbage,
green beans, zucchini, parsley, pesto and salt and pepper to taste. Simmer for
an additional 30 minutes, or until all the vegetables are soft.

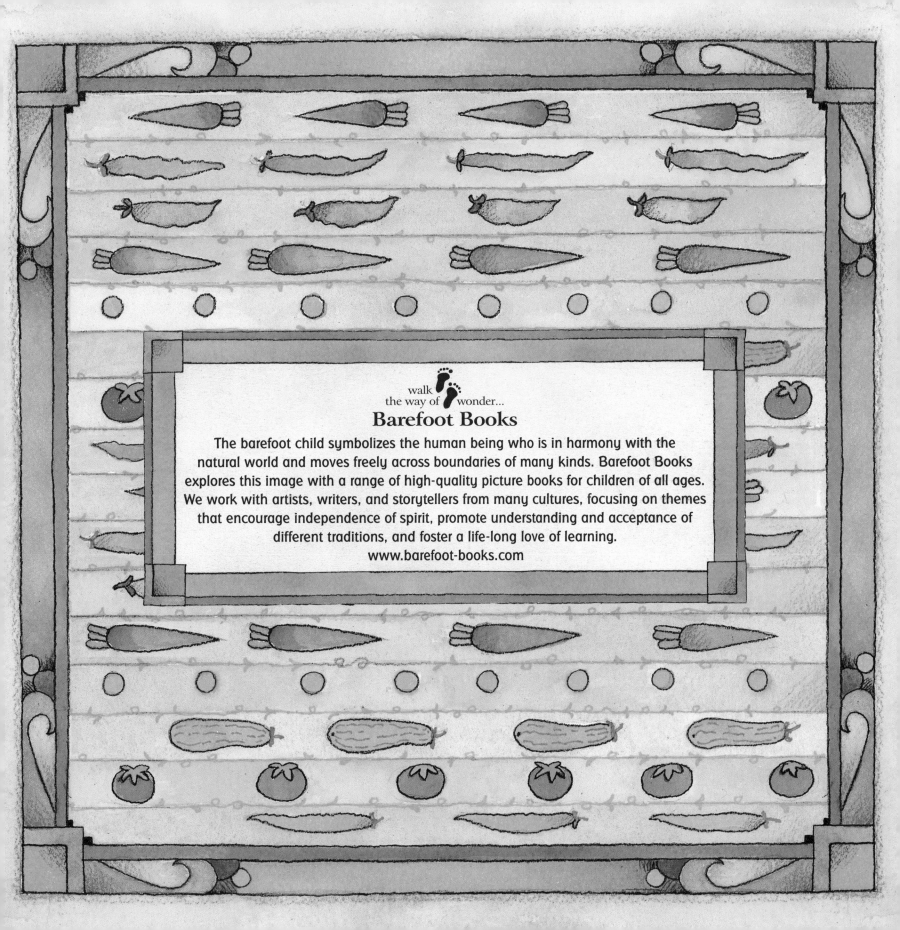

walk
the way of wonder...

Barefoot Books

The barefoot child symbolizes the human being who is in harmony with the natural world and moves freely across boundaries of many kinds. Barefoot Books explores this image with a range of high-quality picture books for children of all ages. We work with artists, writers, and storytellers from many cultures, focusing on themes that encourage independence of spirit, promote understanding and acceptance of different traditions, and foster a life-long love of learning.

www.barefoot-books.com

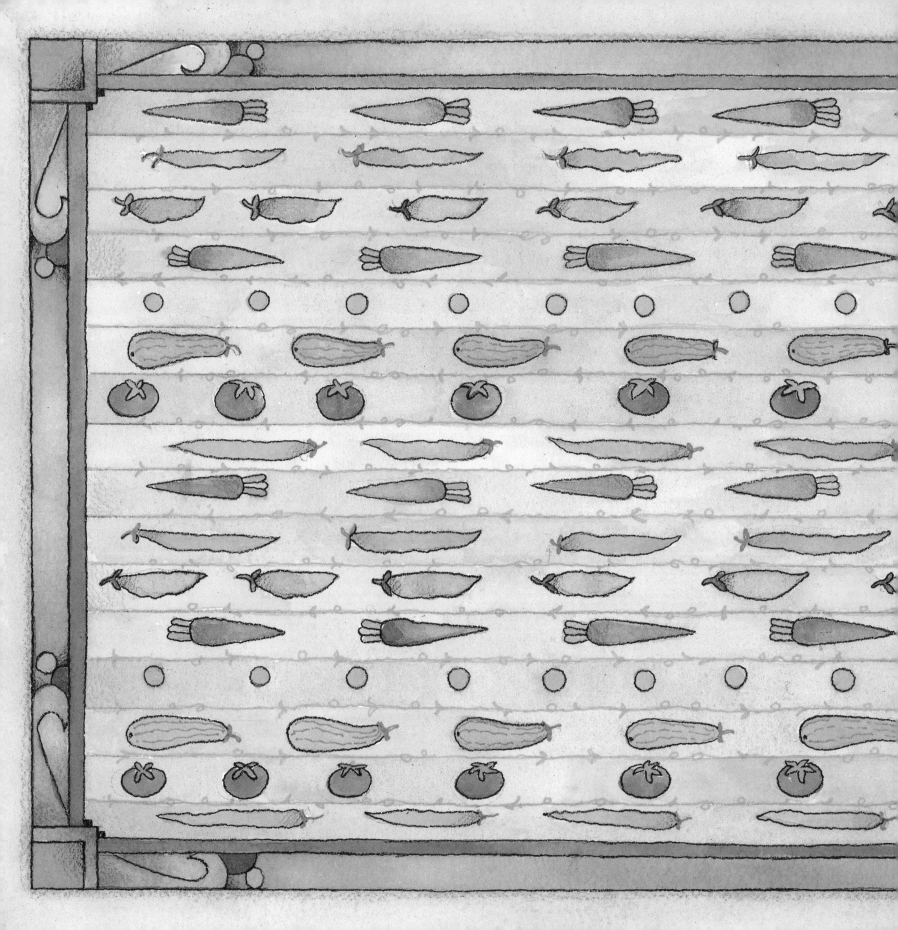